PICTURE WINDOW BOOKS
World Atlases

ATLAS of the
Far East and
Southeast
Asia

by Felicia Law

PICTURE WINDOW BOOKS
Minneapolis, Minnesota

First American edition published in 2008 by
Picture Window Books
5115 Excelsior Boulevard
Suite 232
Minneapolis, MN 55416
877-845-8392
www.picturewindowbooks.com

Editor: Jill Kalz
Designer: Hilary Wacholz
Page Production: Melissa Kes
Art Director: Nathan Gassman
Associate Managing Editor: Christianne Jones
Cartographer: XNR Productions, Inc. (13, 15, 17, 19)

Editor and Compiler: Felicia Law
Research: Trevor Glover
Designers: Fanny Masters & Maia Terry
Picture Researcher: Diana Morris
Illustrators: Rebecca Elliott, Ali Lodge, and Q2 Media
Maps: Geo-Innovations UK

Printed in the United States of America.

All books published by Picture Window Books
are manufactured with paper containing at least
10 percent post-consumer waste.

Law, Felicia.
Atlas of the Far East and Southeast Asia / by Felicia Law. – Minneapolis, MN :
Picture Window Books, 2008.
32 p. : col. ill., col. maps ; cm. – (Picture Window Books world atlases).
2-4
2-4.
Includes index and glossary.
ISBN 978-1-4048-3883-3
1. Maps – Juvenile literature. 2. Asia – Geography – Juvenile literature. 3. Asia – Maps
for children.
DS5.92   915 REF
                                                       DLC

Photo Credits:
Daniel Aguilar/Reuters/Corbis: 12; Bernard Annebicque/Sygma/Corbis: 18tr; Morton Beebe/Corbis: 26bl; Tibor Bognar/Corbis: 21cr; Bohemian Nomad Picturemakers/Corbis: 24c, Kurt de Bruyn/Shutterstock: 20br; Vinai Ditnajohn/epa/Corbis: 21bl; Robert Francis/Robert Harding World Imagery/Corbis: 8bl; Free Agents Ltd/Corbis: 26tr; Stephen Frink/epa/Corbis: 19, 22tr; Getty Images: 21tl; Craig Hansen/Shutterstock: 23bl; Jason Hosking/zefa/Corbis: 6bl; Andrew K/epa/Corbis: 10; Earl & Nazima Kowall/Corbis: 20bl; Kurt/Dreamstime: 4, 7, 9, 11, 13, 15, 17, 19, 25, 27; Jason Maehl/Shutterstock: 8tr; Hugo Maes/Shutterstock: 27; Gunter Marx Photography/Corbis: 6tr; Vladimir Medvedev/Shutterstock: 9b, Zeng Nian/Corbis: 7cr; NOAA/Corbis: 12cl; Thomas Nord/Shutterstock: 22cl; pdtnc/Shutterstock: 23cr; Pictor International/Alamy: 29; Vova Pomortzeff/Shutterstock: 23cl; Radu Razvan/Shutterstock: 20tr; Wendy Shiao/Shutterstock: 18bl; Superbild/Al Pix: 22br; TAOLMOR/Shutterstock: 11, 23tr; Nevada Weir/Corbis: 24tr; Alison Wright/Corbis: 28-29

Editor's Note: The maps in this book were created with the Miller projection.

Table of Contents

Welcome to the Far East and Southeast Asia

The world is made up of five oceans and seven chunks of land called continents: North America, South America, Antarctica, Europe, Africa, Asia, and Australia.

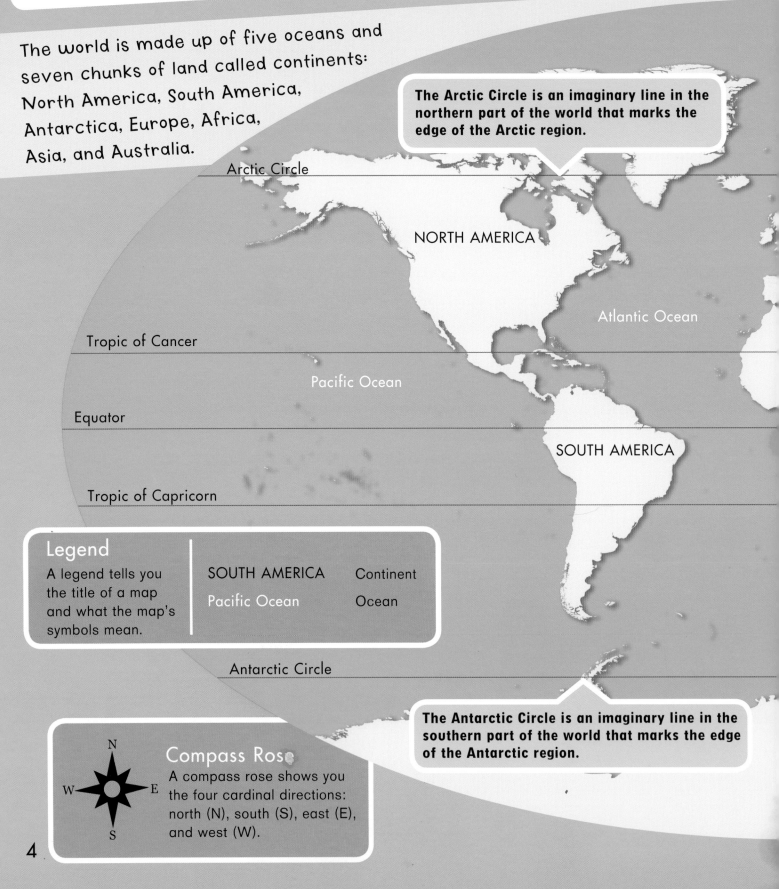

The Arctic Circle is an imaginary line in the northern part of the world that marks the edge of the Arctic region.

Arctic Circle

NORTH AMERICA

Atlantic Ocean

Tropic of Cancer

Pacific Ocean

Equator

SOUTH AMERICA

Tropic of Capricorn

Legend
A legend tells you the title of a map and what the map's symbols mean.

| SOUTH AMERICA | Continent |
| Pacific Ocean | Ocean |

Antarctic Circle

The Antarctic Circle is an imaginary line in the southern part of the world that marks the edge of the Antarctic region.

Compass Rose
A compass rose shows you the four cardinal directions: north (N), south (S), east (E), and west (W).

N
W E
S

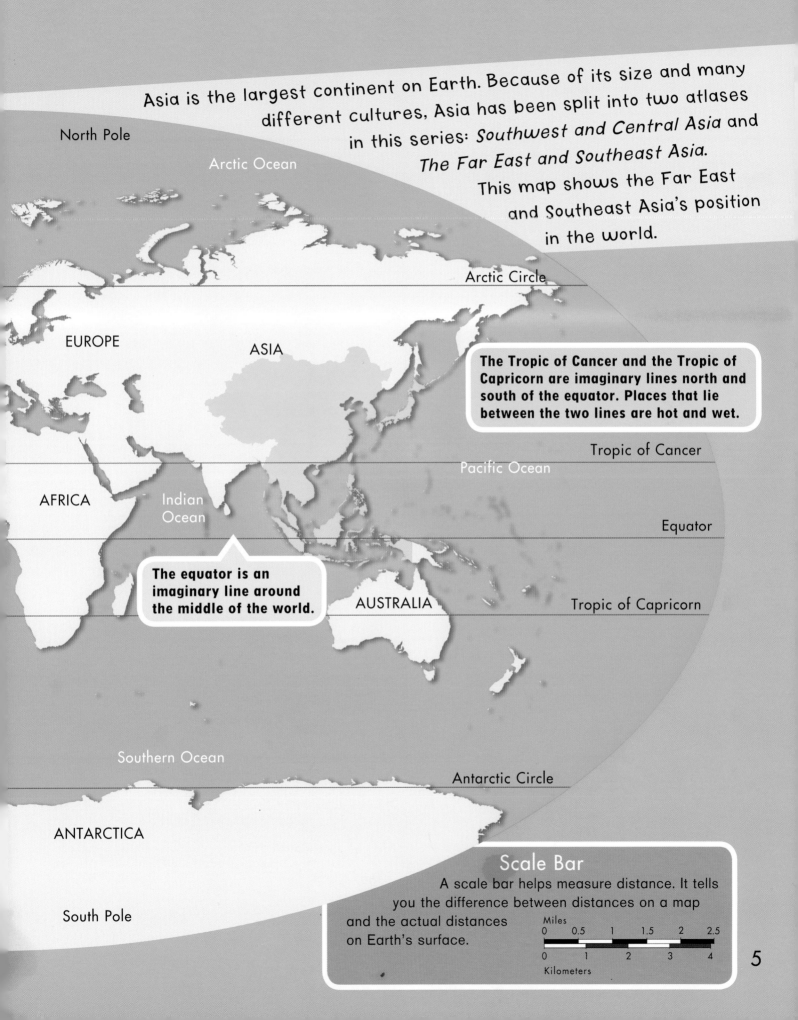

Asia is the largest continent on Earth. Because of its size and many different cultures, Asia has been split into two atlases in this series: *Southwest and Central Asia* and *The Far East and Southeast Asia*. This map shows the Far East and Southeast Asia's position in the world.

North Pole

Arctic Ocean

Arctic Circle

EUROPE

ASIA

The Tropic of Cancer and the Tropic of Capricorn are imaginary lines north and south of the equator. Places that lie between the two lines are hot and wet.

Tropic of Cancer

Pacific Ocean

AFRICA

Indian Ocean

Equator

The equator is an imaginary line around the middle of the world.

AUSTRALIA

Tropic of Capricorn

Southern Ocean

Antarctic Circle

ANTARCTICA

South Pole

Scale Bar

A scale bar helps measure distance. It tells you the difference between distances on a map and the actual distances on Earth's surface.

Miles
0   0.5   1   1.5   2   2.5

0   1   2   3   4
Kilometers

5

Countries

There are 17 countries in the Far East and Southeast Asia. The largest is China. The smallest is Singapore.

These 17 countries, added to those of Southwest and Central Asia, give the continent of Asia a total of 49 countries.

Many languages are spoken throughout the Far East and Southeast Asia, including Japanese, Korean, Bengali, English, and Filipino. But Mandarin Chinese has the largest number of native speakers.

Chinese language

There are many different Chinese languages, but the most used is Mandarin. More than twice as many people in the world speak Mandarin than speak English. Written Chinese can be difficult to learn. English, for example, uses 26 letters in its alphabet. Chinese uses 3,000 to 4,000!

An example of Chinese writing

Having fun

Many Asian families love music and dance. They enjoy hearing and seeing traditional stories at the opera and puppet theaters. Flutes, reed pipes, and lutes (like a small guitar) are common instruments in traditional Asian music.

Japanese drummers putting on a show

What's on the menu?

Japan – tuna, shrimp, or eel sushi

Mongolia – mutton (sheep) dumplings

Philippines – chicken and pork adobo

Singapore – skewered meat with peanut sauce

South Korea – bean sprouts

Thailand – chicken with green curry

Vietnam – chicken and rice noodle soup

BRUNEI   CAMBODIA   CHINA   INDONESIA   JAPAN   NORTH KOREA   SOUTH KOREA

LAOS

MALAYSIA

MONGOLIA

MYANMAR
(BURMA)

MONGOLIA

NORTH
KOREA

SOUTH
KOREA

JAPAN

CHINA

Tropic of Cancer

MYANMAR
(BURMA)

VIETNAM

LAOS

TAIWAN

THAILAND

PHILIPPINES

CAMBODIA

N

W   E

S

Pacific Ocean

BRUNEI

MALAYSIA

SINGAPORE

Miles
0   200   400   600   800   1,000

0   400   800   1,200   1,600
Kilometers

Indian Ocean

INDONESIA

Equator

TIMOR-LESTE (EAST TIMOR)

PHILIPPINES   SINGAPORE   TAIWAN   THAILAND   TIMOR-LESTE
(EAST TIMOR)   VIETNAM

Landforms

The Far East and Southeast Asia region is very mountainous.

Smaller mountains cover many of the region's island countries, including Japan, Indonesia, and the Philippines. Some of the world's tallest mountains are in western China.

Across eastern China lie large areas of flat land called plains. Most people in China live on the plains.

Chocolate Hills

The Chocolate Hills are a famous site in the Philippines. There are 1,268 hills, all the same shape and roughly the same size. They are covered with grass that turns chocolate brown at the end of the summer. The color gives the hills their name.

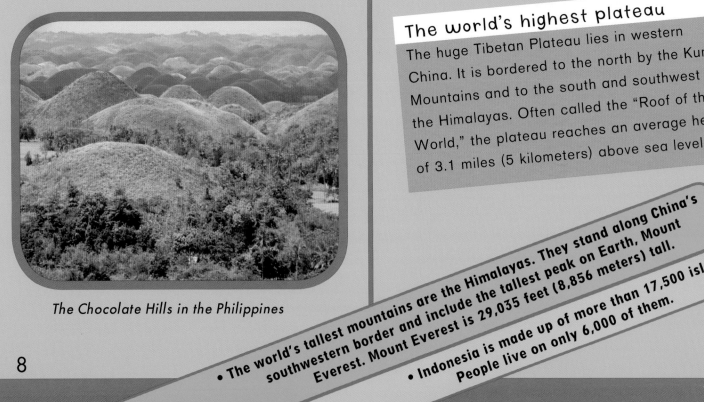

The Chocolate Hills in the Philippines

Ring of Fire

The Ring of Fire is a long chain of volcanoes and earthquake activity that circles much of the Pacific Ocean (see page 28). More than half of the world's volcanoes lie along the Ring of Fire. A volcano is a type of mountain that throws smoke, ash, and red-hot lava high into the air.

Thousands of volcanic mountains rise out of the ocean along the Ring of Fire.

The world's highest plateau

The huge Tibetan Plateau lies in western China. It is bordered to the north by the Kunlun Mountains and to the south and southwest by the Himalayas. Often called the "Roof of the World," the plateau reaches an average height of 3.1 miles (5 kilometers) above sea level.

- The world's tallest mountains are the Himalayas. They stand along China's southwestern border and include the tallest peak on Earth, Mount Everest. Mount Everest is 29,035 feet (8,856 meters) tall.

- Indonesia is made up of more than 17,500 islands. People live on only 6,000 of them.

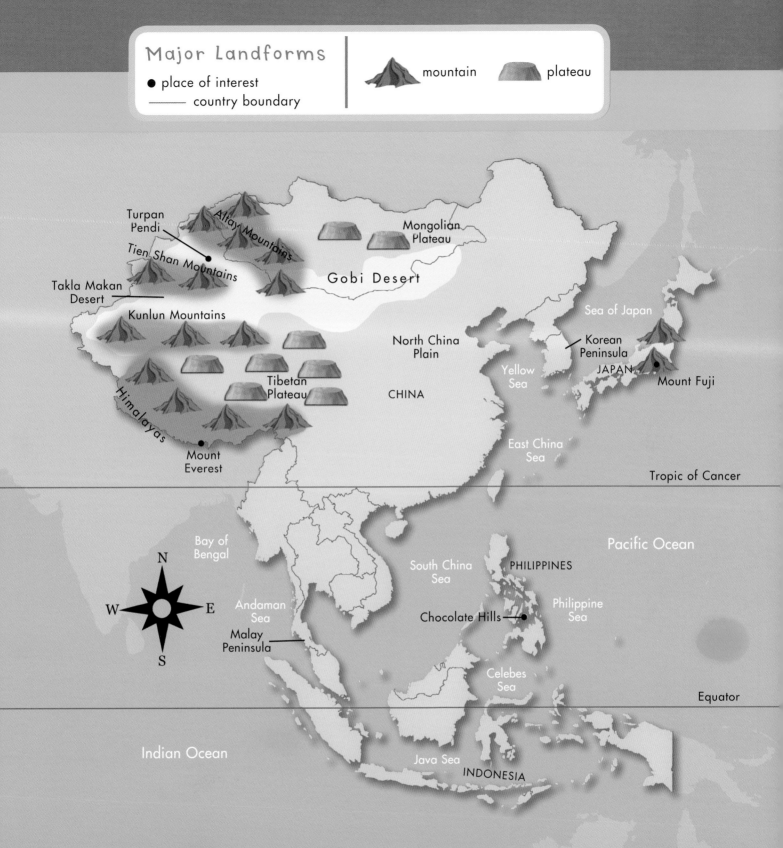

Major Landforms

- ● place of interest
- —— country boundary

🏔 mountain   ⬢ plateau

Turpan Pendi

Altay Mountains

Tien Shan Mountains

Takla Makan Desert

Kunlun Mountains

Himalayas

Mount Everest

Tibetan Plateau

Gobi Desert

Mongolian Plateau

North China Plain

CHINA

Sea of Japan

Korean Peninsula

JAPAN

Yellow Sea

Mount Fuji

East China Sea

Tropic of Cancer

Bay of Bengal

N W E S

Andaman Sea

Malay Peninsula

South China Sea

PHILIPPINES

Chocolate Hills

Philippine Sea

Pacific Ocean

Celebes Sea

Equator

Indian Ocean

Java Sea

INDONESIA

The largest desert in the Far East and Southeast Asia is the Gobi Desert. Deserts are not landforms, but the Gobi is an important part of the region's landscape. Except for some places in the south, much of the Gobi Desert is covered with rocks and gravel.

Large sand dunes in the southern Gobi Desert

9

Bodies of Water

The Far East and Southeast Asia are closely tied to many bodies of water.

Long rivers flow across much of the land. Miles and miles of coastline border a number of seas, including the Yellow Sea, the South China Sea, and the Java Sea.

The seas surrounding the Far East and Southeast Asia are part of the Pacific Ocean and the Indian Ocean.

Three Gorges Dam

Building the Three Gorges Dam across China's Chang Jiang River is one of the world's largest projects. The dam will help control the flooding of the Chang Jiang, which has taken many lives over the years. It will also use the power of the water to create electricity. The project is scheduled to be completed in 2009.

The waters of the Chang Jiang River flow through the Three Gorges Dam.

Pirates ahoy!

Pirates still sail the waters of Southeast Asia. But instead of ships, swords, and cannons, today's pirates use speedboats, guns, and cell phones. The South China Sea is one of the busiest trade routes for shipping in the world. It is also the most dangerous. About 150 pirate attacks take place in its waters each year.

- The Huang (Yellow) River is China's second-longest river. The river gets its name from the yellow, sandy soil carried along by the water.
- The Mekong River starts in western China and ends in the South China Sea. The land surrounding the river's nine mouths makes up the Mekong Delta.
- The Irrawaddy River flows through the center of Myanmar. It is the country's most important waterway.

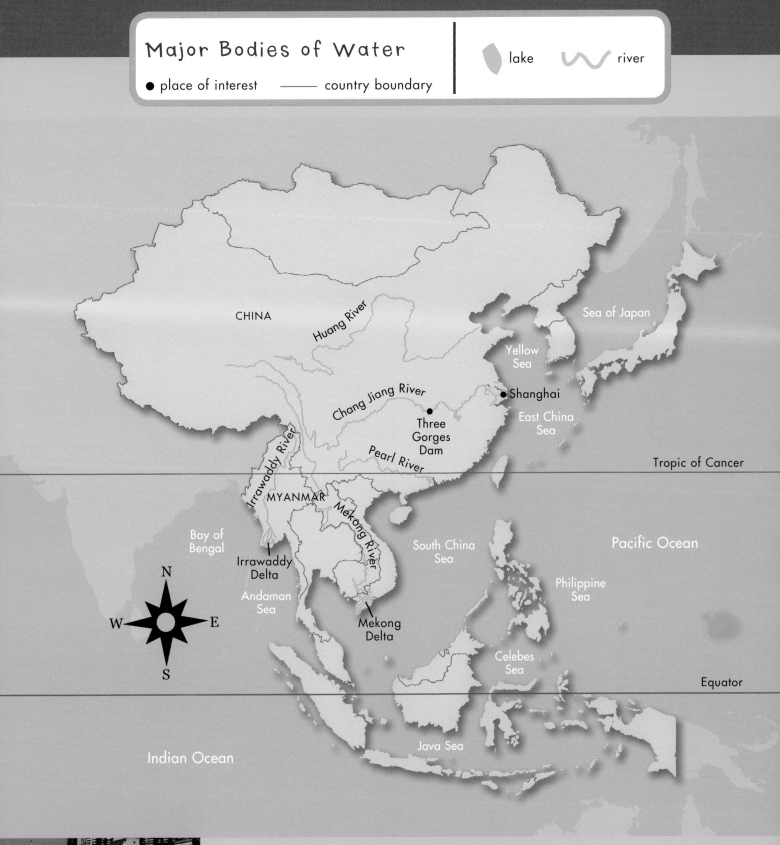

Major Bodies of Water

● place of interest ——— country boundary

lake ⬗ ～ river

CHINA

Huang River

Chang Jiang River

Three Gorges Dam

Pearl River

Irrawaddy River

MYANMAR

Mekong River

Bay of Bengal

Irrawaddy Delta

Andaman Sea

Mekong Delta

N W E S

Sea of Japan

Yellow Sea

● Shanghai

East China Sea

Tropic of Cancer

South China Sea

Pacific Ocean

Philippine Sea

Celebes Sea

Equator

Java Sea

Indian Ocean

The Chang Jiang River (also called the Yangtze) is the longest river in China and the third-longest river in the world. It flows through steep valleys toward the sea. Its wide mouth lies near the city of Shanghai.

The Chang Jiang River is busy with boat traffic.

11

Climate

Climate is the average weather a place has from season to season, year to year. Rainfall and temperature play large parts in a region's climate.

While most of the countries near the equator and the Tropic of Cancer have a tropical climate, countries farther north have a wider range.

China is such a huge country that five different types of climates can be found there: dry, continental, mountain, mild, and tropical.

El Niño

El Niño is the nickname for a strange weather pattern that hits many southern parts of the world every two to seven years. Scientists believe it is caused by an unusual warming of the Pacific Ocean off the coast of Indonesia. During El Niño years, storms, droughts (times of no rain), and floods are common.

Monsoon seasons

The monsoons are strong winds that blow off the Indian Ocean and the South China Sea. These winds bring two seasons, known as the monsoon seasons. Monsoon seasons are marked by heavy rainfall and tropical windstorms called hurricanes.

Gusty winds blow during the monsoon seasons.

Climate basics

A region's climate depends upon three major things: how close it is to the ocean, how high up it is, and how close it is to the equator. Areas along the ocean have milder climates than areas farther inland. The higher a region is, and the farther it is from the equator, the colder its temperature.

- Indonesia receives an average of 7 to 11 inches (18 to 28 centimeters) of rain each month. The heaviest amounts fall during the wet season—November to April.

- Winter in Mongolia is long and cold. The average winter temperature is minus 4 degrees Fahrenheit (minus 20 degrees Celsius). Some nights can dip down to minus 40 F (minus 40 C).

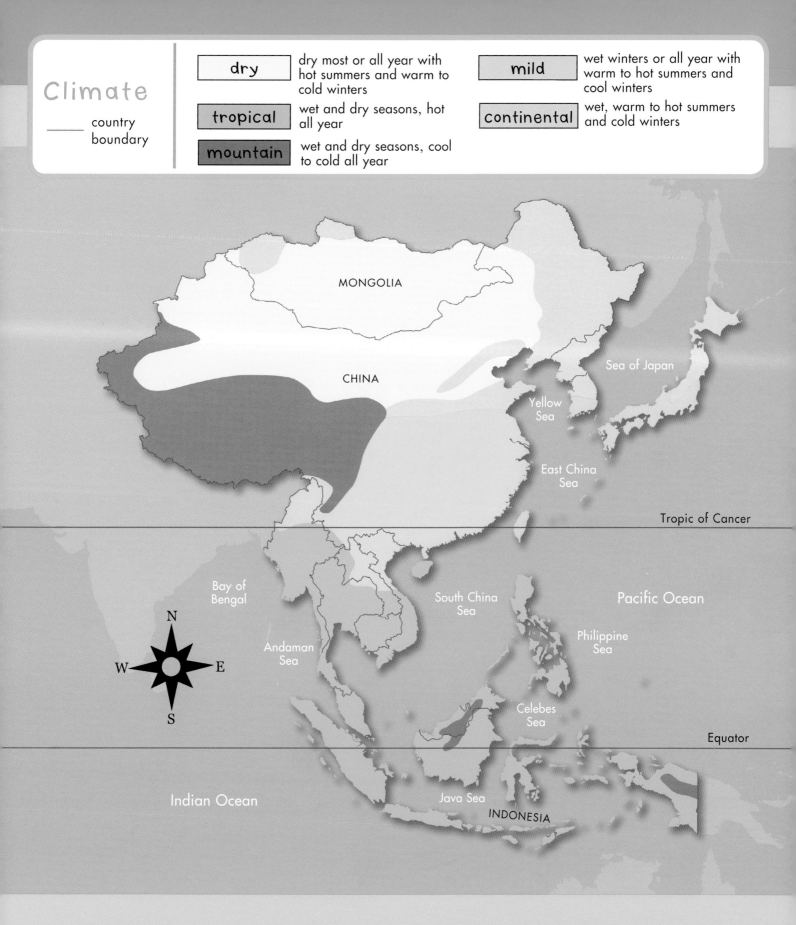

Climate

_____ country boundary

dry	dry most or all year with hot summers and warm to cold winters
tropical	wet and dry seasons, hot all year
mountain	wet and dry seasons, cool to cold all year
mild	wet winters or all year with warm to hot summers and cool winters
continental	wet, warm to hot summers and cold winters

MONGOLIA

CHINA

Sea of Japan

Yellow Sea

East China Sea

Tropic of Cancer

Bay of Bengal

Pacific Ocean

South China Sea

Philippine Sea

N

W   E

S

Andaman Sea

Celebes Sea

Equator

Indian Ocean

Java Sea

INDONESIA

Plants

Plants in the Far East and Southeast Asia are well-adapted to the region's many ecosystems, including deserts, grasslands, rain forests, and mountains. An ecosystem is all of the living and nonliving things in a certain area. It includes plants, animals, soil, weather ... everything!

The rain forests of Southeast Asia are like large, layered greenhouses. The top layers get a lot of sunlight, while the layers along the forest floor get very little. Some plants, such as vines, adapt to these conditions by climbing trees to reach the sunlight.

Some Plants of the Far East and Southeast Asia

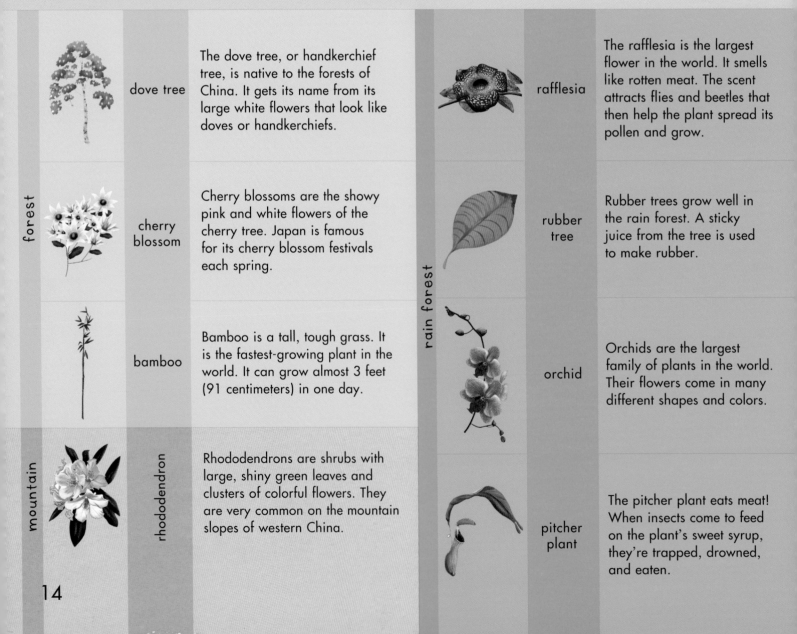

forest

dove tree — The dove tree, or handkerchief tree, is native to the forests of China. It gets its name from its large white flowers that look like doves or handkerchiefs.

cherry blossom — Cherry blossoms are the showy pink and white flowers of the cherry tree. Japan is famous for its cherry blossom festivals each spring.

bamboo — Bamboo is a tall, tough grass. It is the fastest-growing plant in the world. It can grow almost 3 feet (91 centimeters) in one day.

mountain

rhododendron — Rhododendrons are shrubs with large, shiny green leaves and clusters of colorful flowers. They are very common on the mountain slopes of western China.

rain forest

rafflesia — The rafflesia is the largest flower in the world. It smells like rotten meat. The scent attracts flies and beetles that then help the plant spread its pollen and grow.

rubber tree — Rubber trees grow well in the rain forest. A sticky juice from the tree is used to make rubber.

orchid — Orchids are the largest family of plants in the world. Their flowers come in many different shapes and colors.

pitcher plant — The pitcher plant eats meat! When insects come to feed on the plant's sweet syrup, they're trapped, drowned, and eaten.

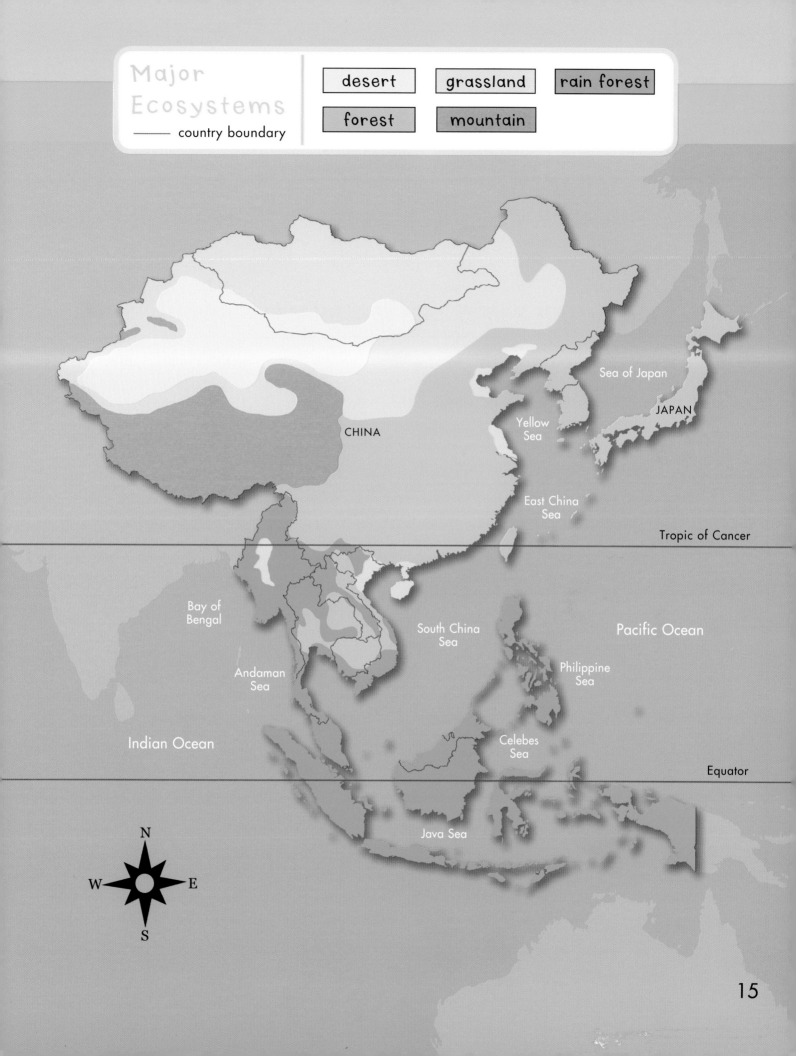

Major Ecosystems

—— country boundary

desert   grassland   rain forest

forest   mountain

CHINA

JAPAN

Sea of Japan

Yellow
Sea

East China
Sea

Tropic of Cancer

Bay of
Bengal

South China
Sea

Pacific Ocean

Andaman
Sea

Philippine
Sea

Indian Ocean

Celebes
Sea

Equator

Java Sea

N
W   E
S

Animals

Many different kinds of animals live in the Far East and Southeast Asia. All are well-adapted to the ecosystems in which they live. An ecosystem is all of the living and nonliving things in a certain area.

Animals of the Far East and Southeast Asia include mammals such as camels, elephants, and leopards; birds such as cranes, ducks, and parrots; reptiles such as snakes and turtles; many kinds of fish; and thousands of insect species.

Some Animals of the Far East and Southeast Asia

desert	Bactrian camel	The Bactrian camel has two humps. The humps are filled with fat, not water. The camel uses the fat whenever there is little water or food.	**rain forest**	Sumatran rhinoceros	Sumatran rhinoceroses are the smallest and rarest rhinos in the world. Most of them live on the island of Sumatra.
forest	giant panda	Wild giant pandas are found only in a few forests in central China. Bamboo makes up 99 percent of their diet.		orangutan	Orangutans spend most of their lives in trees. They use their long arms to swing from branch to branch.
	Asian elephant	The Asian elephant weighs less than the African elephant, has smaller ears, and has two bumps on its forehead.	**grassland**	Komodo dragon	The Komodo dragon is the largest lizard in the world. It lives only on small patches of grassland on a few Indonesian islands.
	flying lizard	The flying lizard can extend its limbs to make "wings" and glide between trees.	**mountain**	snow leopard	The snow leopard's fur is long and woolly. It helps protect the cat in cold weather.
	water buffalo	People use water buffalo for meat, milk, and the plowing work they do.		Pallas' cat	The Pallas' cat is about the size of a housecat. It feeds mostly on small, rabbit-like animals called pikas.
	red-crowned crane	One of the largest breeding areas for red-crowned cranes is northern Japan.		Tibetan yak	Tibetan yaks have large lungs. They help the animals breathe easier in the thin mountain air.

16

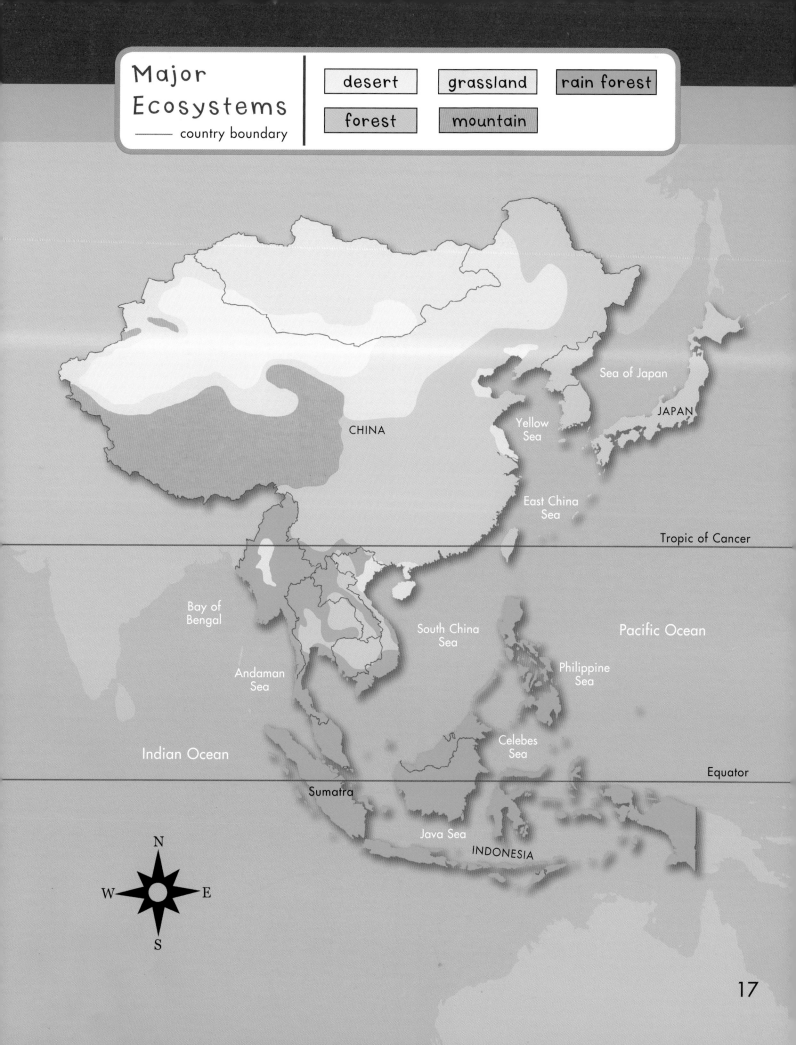

Major
Ecosystems
—— country boundary

desert   grassland   rain forest
forest   mountain

CHINA

Sea of Japan

JAPAN

Yellow
Sea

East China
Sea

Tropic of Cancer

Bay of
Bengal

South China
Sea

Pacific Ocean

Philippine
Sea

Andaman
Sea

Indian Ocean

Celebes
Sea

Equator

Sumatra

Java Sea

INDONESIA

N
W   E
S

Population

Large numbers of people in the Far East and Southeast Asia live near the coasts. The oceans are a source of jobs, food, and fun.

Large numbers of people also live on the plains of China. The land and climate there are perfect for growing crops.

China has 20 percent of the world's population. The Far East and Southeast Asia is where the world's population is growing fastest. By the year 2050, 60 percent of all of the people on Earth will be living in Asia.

Four big cities

Tokyo is the capital of Japan. With 35 million people in the city and surrounding area, Tokyo is the most-populated city in the world. It is a center of international business.

The streets of Tokyo are very crowded.

Nearly 10 million people live in **Seoul**, the capital of South Korea. That number is about one-fourth of South Korea's total population.

Shanghai is the most-populated city in China. Almost 13 million people live there. Once a sleepy fishing town, Shanghai has become China's fastest-growing city. Some of the tallest buildings in the world are found in Shanghai.

Jakarta, Indonesia, is home to more than 12 million people. It is the country's capital, largest port city, and center of transportation and industry.

People!

More people live in China than in any other country in the world. About 1.3 billion people live there. More than one-fourth of them are younger than 14 years old. The capital city is Beijing. The city and the surrounding area is home to nearly 11 million people.

A Chinese girl

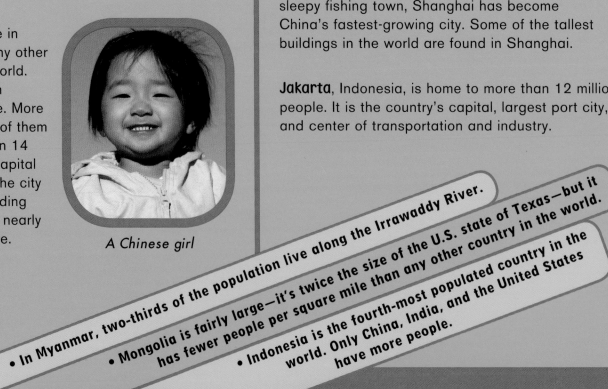

- In Myanmar, two-thirds of the population live along the Irrawaddy River.
- Mongolia is fairly large—it's twice the size of the U.S. state of Texas—but it has fewer people per square mile than any other country in the world.
- Indonesia is the fourth-most populated country in the world. Only China, India, and the United States have more people.

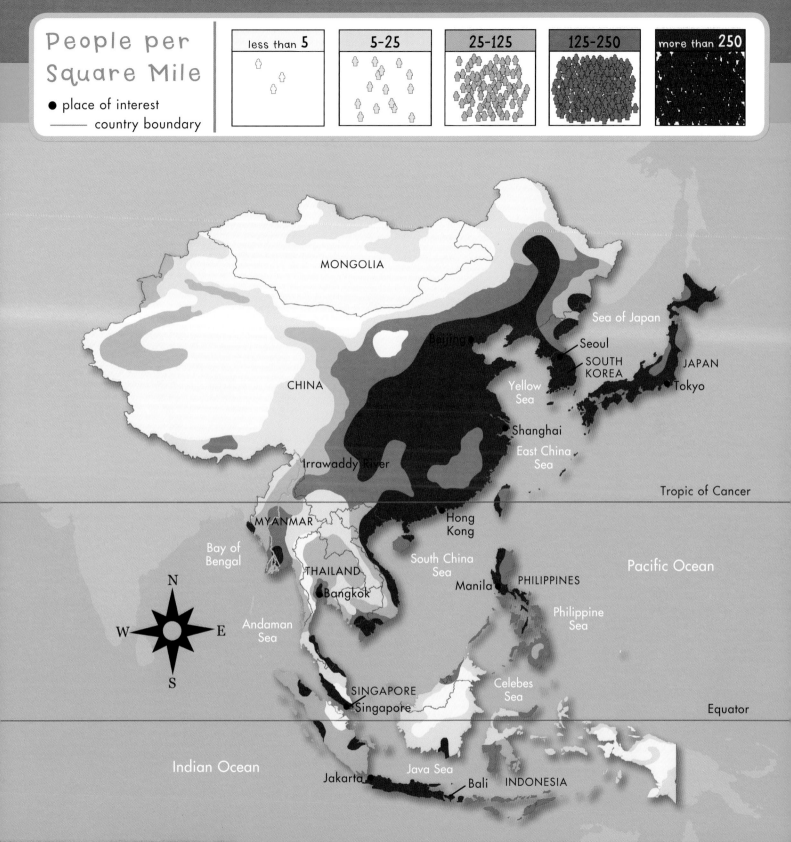

People per Square Mile

- **●** place of interest
- — country boundary

less than 5	5-25	25-125	125-250	more than 250

MONGOLIA

CHINA

Beijing

Irrawaddy River

Sea of Japan

Seoul
SOUTH KOREA

Yellow Sea

JAPAN
Tokyo

Shanghai
East China Sea

Tropic of Cancer

MYANMAR

Bay of Bengal

THAILAND
Bangkok

Andaman Sea

Hong Kong

South China Sea

Manila PHILIPPINES

Philippine Sea

Pacific Ocean

N
W   E
S

SINGAPORE
Singapore

Celebes Sea

Equator

Indian Ocean

Jakarta   Java Sea
Bali   INDONESIA

The beautiful islands of Southeast Asia attract many tourists. These visitors can double the size of the islands' population. The island of Bali, Indonesia, is home to 3 million people. But it welcomes another 3 million people as tourists each year.

People in Bali, Indonesia, enjoy warm weather, sandy beaches, and colorful sunsets.

19

People and Customs

Asia has more people than any other continent in the world.

The people of the Far East and Southeast Asia share some of the same traditions and religious beliefs. But they also have many customs that set their countries apart and make them special.

The countries' different languages, foods, sports, and art forms make the region an exciting place to live.

Festival days

Each country has special holidays and festivals. In Japan, for example, every May 5th is Children's Day. On this day, children fly kites. Many of the kites are shaped like a type of fish called a carp. One carp kite flies for each child in the family.

Japanese fish kites

Mountain people

The Ifugao people live in the mountains of the Philippines. They keep themselves separate from other Filipinos, living as farmers. They even have their own languages. The Ifugao are famous for the terraced (stepped) rice fields they carve into the steep mountain slopes.

An Ifugao woman wears colorful headwear decorated with bird feathers.

Religion

One thing many of the people in the Far East and Southeast Asia share is religion. Buddhism is one of the world's major religions and the one practiced by most people in Asia. Buddhist monks wear robes of orange-colored cloth and live a simple life of prayer.

A gathering of Buddhist monks

Martial arts

Most people think that karate, judo, and other martial arts came from old East Asian cultures. But many are based on ancient fighting skills brought from all over the world. People use martial arts for fighting and self-defense. They also practice them as a sport.

Karate athletes

What's cooking?

What people eat is often tied to where they live. Most people in the Far East and Southeast Asia eat rice because it grows well in the region's warm, wet climate. They also enjoy a lot of seafood because of the region's many coasts and islands.

Asian street vendors preparing meals

Carrying royalty

The Subanahongsa is a swan-like barge (a large, flat-bottomed boat). It has been used on special days by the royal family of Thailand for more than 300 years. The Subanahongsa was made from the trunk of a single teak tree.

The royal barge of Thailand

Postcard Places

The Far East and Southeast Asia have many wonderful places to visit. Not surprisingly, the people who live in this region are the people who visit its exciting sites the most!

Philippines

One of China's most exciting cities is Hong Kong. The name Hong Kong means "fragrant harbor." A harbor is a protected place along a coast.

Hong Kong by night

In the Philippines, many houses are built high on stilts to keep them dry when the seasonal floods come. Steep roofs help the heavy rains drain away.

Great Wall of China

CHINA

Mount Fuji

Hong Kong

Yangon

Bangkok

PHILIPPINES

Year of the Dragon

The Chinese celebrate their New Year with lively, colorful parades through the streets.

Shwedagon Pagoda

The Shwedagon Pagoda sits in the heart of Yangon, Myanmar. It is just one of many thousands of Buddhist monuments in the Far East and Southeast Asia. Buddhism is one of the world's major religions. Many people in Asia are Buddhist.

The Damnoen Saduak floating market outside Bangkok, Thailand, is unusual. Vendors sell fresh fruits and vegetables from boats floating on the water.

Floating Markets

THE GREAT WALL

The Great Wall of China winds 4,000 miles (6,400 kilometers) across the country. It is one of the longest man-made structures in the world.

Mount Fuji

The highest point in Japan is a volcano called Mount Fuji. It is 12,388 feet (3,778 meters) tall and thought by many people to be a holy mountain. Mount Fuji last erupted (threw ash and hot, melted rock into the air) 300 years ago.

23

Rice is one of the most important crops in the world. And more of it is grown in the Far East and Southeast Asia than anywhere else on Earth.

In addition to agriculture, the region has many other industries, including fishing, clothing, mining, and manufacturing. Japan is well-known for the cars it makes.

Woodworking

Hardwood trees produce wood that is very good for carving. Teak is a type of hardwood tree. Myanmar is one of the only countries in the world where teak trees grow naturally. As a result, Myanmar is a major exporter of teak and carved teak furniture.

Carving a piece of teak furniture

Growing rice

Rice is usually planted by hand in paddies. Paddies are shallow, soggy fields. Once the rice is ripe, it is usually harvested by hand, too.

Planting rice by hand is hard work.

Raising animals

Nearly half of Mongolia's workers raise animals, mostly sheep and goats. Live animals and animal products make up 90 percent of Mongolia's exports.

Fishing the seas

The seas around the Far East and Southeast Asia are full of fish. Japan has one of the largest fishing fleets in the world. Tuna is a large fish that is caught off the coasts of Japan and Taiwan. Sharks are caught around Indonesia.

- Thailand and Vietnam are the top two rice exporters in the world. Together, they export almost half of the world's rice.
- Brunei has a lot of oil and natural gas, which it exports all over the world.
- The Philippines is the world's largest exporter of coconuts and coconut oil.

Major Natural Resources, Land Use, and Industry

Manufacturing
Ranching
Mining
Farming

Forestry
Natural Gas
metal
rice

Oil
Fishing
coal
coconuts

Clothing
Technology
nuts

—— country boundary

MONGOLIA

CHINA

JAPAN

MYANMAR

THAILAND

VIETNAM

TAIWAN

Tropic of Cancer

PHILIPPINES

Pacific Ocean

BRUNEI

Indian Ocean

Equator

INDONESIA

N
W E
S

25

Transportation

Transportation in the Far East and Southeast Asia can be a challenge. The region's mountains, plateaus, deserts, and many, many islands make it hard to get around.

Trains, buses, and bikes are the most common methods of transportation on land. The fastest way to travel between islands is by plane.

Large ships carry goods to and from port cities on the Indian Ocean and Pacific Ocean.

Setting sail

Traditional wooden sailing ships still carry goods around the islands of Indonesia and the Philippines. Many of these tall-masted boats are fitted with engines. They also have comfortable living spaces for tourists and other travelers.

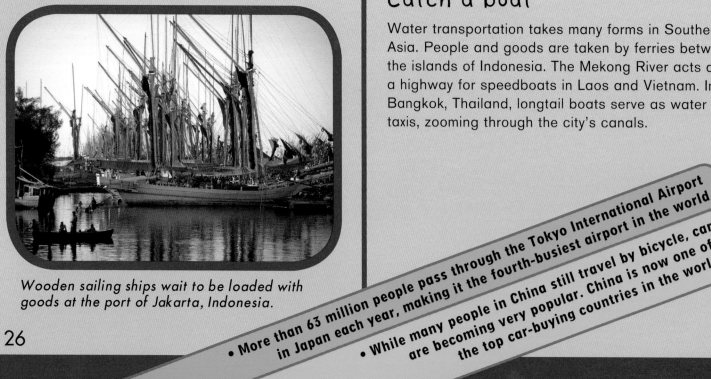

Wooden sailing ships wait to be loaded with goods at the port of Jakarta, Indonesia.

High-speed trains

High-speed "bullet" trains run on a network of tracks that connect Tokyo with most of Japan's other major cities. When the train started in 1964, it was the world's first high-speed train. Today, bullet trains, or *shinkansen*, reach speeds of more than 190 miles (304 kilometers) an hour.

A bullet train zooms through eastern Japan.

Catch a boat

Water transportation takes many forms in Southeast Asia. People and goods are taken by ferries between the islands of Indonesia. The Mekong River acts as a highway for speedboats in Laos and Vietnam. In Bangkok, Thailand, longtail boats serve as water taxis, zooming through the city's canals.

- More than 63 million people pass through the Tokyo International Airport in Japan each year, making it the fourth-busiest airport in the world.
- While many people in China still travel by bicycle, cars are becoming very popular. China is now one of the top car-buying countries in the world.

Major Transportation Routes

● place of interest ——— country boundary

——— major waterway ——— major railroad ——— major highway

CHINA

Huang River

Mekong River

Chang Jiang River

Pearl River

Irrawaddy River

SOUTH KOREA

● Qingdao
● Pusan

JAPAN

● Tokyo

● Shanghai

Tropic of Cancer

TAIWAN
● Kaohsiung

VIETNAM

LAOS

THAILAND

Yangon (Rangoon)

● Bangkok

Hong Kong

Manila ●
PHILIPPINES

Pacific Ocean

N
W   E
S

SINGAPORE
● Singapore

Equator

Indian Ocean

Jakarta ●

INDONESIA

At one time, there were many American soldiers posted near Manila, Philippines. The soldiers' old jeeps were often sold to the local people, who painted them and used them as buses. The buses are called jeepneys.

A painted jeepney on a Filipino street

27

Sailing Around the Pacific Islands

The Ring of Fire is a chain of special islands. It stretches thousands of miles, through Southeast Asia and across the Pacific Ocean to the western coasts of North America and South America. Many of the islands have volcanoes. The white line on this map shows the western edge of the Ring of Fire.

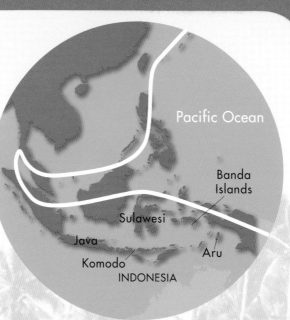

Pacific Ocean

Banda Islands

Sulawesi

Java

Komodo

INDONESIA

Aru

The black-sailed ship pulls away from the Indonesian island of Sulawesi. The ship, called a Phinisi, is a traditional wooden boat of the islanders. Today it is off on a sea trip, carrying some excited passengers. They stand on deck and look out across the water. The captain tells them to keep their eyes open for playful dolphins.

The ship's first stop is the neighboring Banda Islands. The passengers visit the spice markets. They buy bags of nutmeg to take home.

After this short stop, the ship is off to the island of Aru. There, divers search the coral reef for pearls. Only one in every 50,000 mussel shells holds a valuable pearl, but the passengers may buy some of the shells. The colorful shells can be made into beautiful jewelry and ornaments.

The Phinisi now sets sail for the island of Komodo. The passengers must be careful there. Giant Komodo dragons prowl the shore. No one wants to get in the way of the lizards' sharp claws and teeth. These huge lizards eat small animals such as goats and young deer.

The last stop for the passengers will be the island of Java. They can't wait to explore its temples and jungles. The Phinisi, on the other hand, will travel on. It has work to do, helping islanders haul goods from one island to another.

A Phinisi ship sets sail in the waters of Southeast Asia.

The Far East and Southeast Asia At-a-Glance

Continent size: Asia, as a whole, is the largest of Earth's seven continents

Number of countries: 17 in the region, 49 total in Asia

Major languages:
- Burmese
- Chinese Mandarin
- English
- Filipino
- Japanese
- Khmer
- Korean
- Lao
- Malay
- Thai
- Vietnamese

Total population: 2.1 billion in the region, 4 billion total in Asia (2007 estimate)

Largest country (land size): China

Most populated country: China

Most populated city: Tokyo, Japan

Climate: mostly dry with hot summers and cold winters in the North; continental (wet, warm to hot summers and cold winters) in the Northeast; cool to cold in the mountains of the West; mild in the East; tropical in the South

Highest point: Mount Everest, Nepal/China, 29,035 feet (8,856 meters)

Lowest point: Turpan Pendi, China, 505 feet (154 m) below sea level

Longest river: Chang Jiang (Yangtze) River

Largest desert: Gobi Desert

Major agricultural products:
- barley
- cassava
- coconuts
- corn
- cotton
- jute
- palm oil
- rice
- rubber
- soybeans
- sugarcane
- tea
- tobacco
- wheat

Major industries:
- agriculture
- fishing
- mining
- manufacturing (clothing, food and beverage, and electronic equipment)

Natural resources:
- coal
- copper
- gold
- iron
- lead
- oil
- tin

Glossary

body of water – a mass of water that is in one area; such as a river, lake, or ocean

boundary – a line that shows the border of a country, state, or other land area

canal – a waterway dug across land

climate – the average weather a place has from season to season, year to year

compass rose – a symbol used to show direction on a map

continent – one of seven large land masses on Earth, including Africa, Antarctica, Asia, Australia, Europe, North America, and South America

crops – plants that are grown in large amounts and are used for food or income

delta – the land at the mouth of a river; deltas are often shaped like triangles

desert – a hot or cold, very dry area that has few plants growing on it

dune – a hill of sand piled up by the wind

ecosystem – all of the living and nonliving things in a certain area, including plants, animals, soil, and weather

equator – an imaginary line around Earth; it divides the northern and southern hemispheres

export – to send goods to another country to be sold or traded

forest – land covered by trees and plants

forestry – the work of growing and caring for forests

grassland – land covered mostly with grass

island – land that is completely surrounded by water

lake – a body of water that is completely surrounded by land

landform – a natural feature on Earth's surface

legend – the part of a map that explains the meaning of the map's symbols

monsoon – a strong wind that blows across southern Asia and the Indian Ocean

mountain – a mass of land that rises high above the land that surrounds it

natural resources – materials such as water, trees, and minerals that are found in nature

North Pole – the northern-most point on Earth

ocean – the large body of saltwater that covers most of Earth's surface

peninsula – a body of land that is surrounded by water on three sides

plain – an area of flat or nearly flat land

plateau – a large, flat, and often rocky area of land that is higher than the surrounding land

population – the total number of people who live in one area

port – a place where ships can load or unload cargo (goods or people)

rain forest – a thick forest that receives a lot of rain year-round

ranching – the work of raising animals such as cattle and sheep on a ranch

river – a large stream of water that empties into a lake, ocean, or other river

scale – the size of a map or model compared to the actual size of things they stand for

South Pole – the southern-most point on Earth

species – groups of animals or plants that have many things in common

temperature – how hot or cold something is

Index

On the Web

FactHound offers a safe, fun way to find Web sites related to topics in this book.
All of the sites on FactHound have been researched by our staff.

1. Visit *www.facthound.com*
2. Type in this special code: 140483883X
3. Click on the FETCH IT button.

Your trusty FactHound will fetch the best sites for you!

Look for all of the books in the Picture Window Books World Atlases series:

Atlas of Africa
Atlas of Australia
Atlas of Europe
Atlas of North America
Atlas of South America
Atlas of Southwest and Central Asia
Atlas of the Far East and Southeast Asia
Atlas of the Poles and Oceans